W9-CSQ-240

Book 1

Remembrance Day

Jill Foran

Weigl

CALGARY

Published by Weigl Educational Publishers Limited
6325 – 10 Street SE
Calgary, Alberta, Canada
T2H 2Z9
Web site: www.weigl.com

National Library of Canada Cataloguing in Publication Data
Foran, Jill
    Remembrance day

(Canadian holidays)
Includes index.
ISBN 1-894705-95-5

    1. Remembrance Day--Canada--Juvenile literature. I. Title.
II. Series: Canadian holidays (Calgary, Alta.)
D680.C2F67 2002   j394.264   C2002-900815-8

We acknowledge the financial support of the Government of Canada through the Book Publishing
Industry Development Program (BPIDP) for our publishing activities.

Printed in the United States of America
1 2 3 4 5 6 7 8 9 0   06 05 04 03 02

Project Coordinator Heather Kissock **Design** Warren Clark
Copy Editor Jennifer Nault **Layout** Bryan Pezzi **Photo Researcher** Nicole Bezic King

Photo Credits

Cover: www.viewCalgary.com; **Courtesy of the Canadian Forces:** pages 14T, 17T (Sgt MJ Reid), 19BL (Cpl MFC
Morrissette); **www.canadianheritage.org ID# 20941, H.G. Aikman/National Archives of Canada/PA-132651:** page
9T; **Corel Corporation:** pages 4, 17B; **Richard Desmarais:** pages 15M, 15B; **Glenbow Archives:** pages 7T (NA-969-4), 8
(NA-2365-109); **Lloyd Henderson:** page 18L; **Heather Kissock:** pages 15T, 20, 21; **Lone Pine Photo:** pages 3 (Clarence
W. Norris), 5B (Eva Anthony), 13 (Clarence W. Norris), 18M (Clarence W. Norris), 18R (Clarence W. Norris), 19T (Clarence W.
Norris); **National Archives of Canada:** pages 5T (W.I. Castle/PA-832), 6 (W. Rider-Rider/Canada. Dept. of National
Defence/PA-2156), 7B (Canada. Dept. of National Defence/PA-003547), 9B (Canada. Dept. of National Defence/PA-
132651), 12L (W. Rider-Rider/Canada. Dept of National Defence/PA-001918), 12R (C-046284), 16L (PA-066815), 16R
(Canada. Dept of National Defence/PA-129070; **PhotoSpin, Inc.:** page 19BR; **Unité de Photographie des FC CF
Photographic Unit (Rec94-2330-4):** page 10L; **Courtesy Veterans Affairs Canada, Pacific Region:** page 14B;
www.viewCalgary.com: pages 10R, 11, 22.

Contents

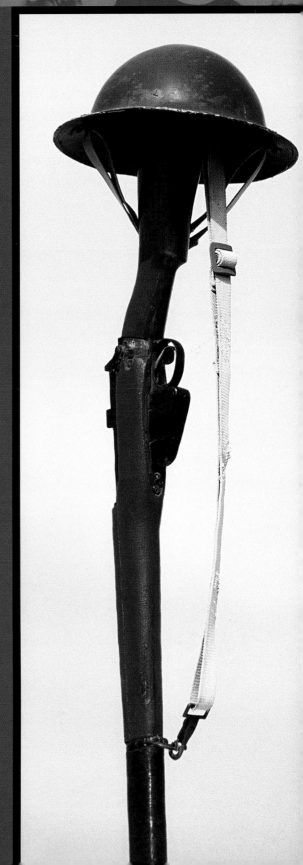

Introduction

This is a time to pay tribute to war veterans.

November 11 is Remembrance Day. This is the day when Canadians honour the men and women who served in World War I, World War II, the Korean War, and various **peacekeeping** missions. Remembrance Day is also a time for Canadians to pay tribute to war **veterans**, and to think about the importance of peace and freedom in their lives.

Since 1956, thousands of Canadians have served in peacekeeping missions all over the world. More than 100 have died while trying to maintain peace.

Canadians live in a free country. This means that they have the right to voice their ideas and opinions. They also have the right to practice their own religion, and to participate in Canada's system of government. Over the years, thousands of Canadians have volunteered to go to war to protect Canada's freedom. Many **sacrificed** their lives for the freedom of their country. Remembrance Day is a time to **commemorate** and give thanks to all those who have served to protect Canada's freedom.

More than 116,000 Canadians died while serving in World War I, World War II, and the Korean War.

Some Remembrance Day ceremonies include military parades and bands.

The Great War

In 1914, a war broke out in Europe.

In 1914, a war broke out in Europe. This war was called the Great War because it was the first time in history that almost every country in the world was involved. Today, the Great War is better known as World War I. Almost 620,000 Canadians served in World War I. They endured terrible hardships, and many were badly injured or killed.

Dirty, cramped conditions and poor nutrition brought deadly diseases to the trenches.

After four long years of battle, World War I came to an end. A peace document was signed. The document, called an **armistice**, stated that all fighting would stop at 11:00 AM on November 11, 1918. Everyone was relieved, but no one wanted to forget the many victims who had died while defending their country. People thought that it would be a good idea to remember these soldiers every November 11. As a result, the first Remembrance Day was held on November 11, 1919. At that time, it was known as Armistice Day. The name of the holiday was officially changed to Remembrance Day in 1931.

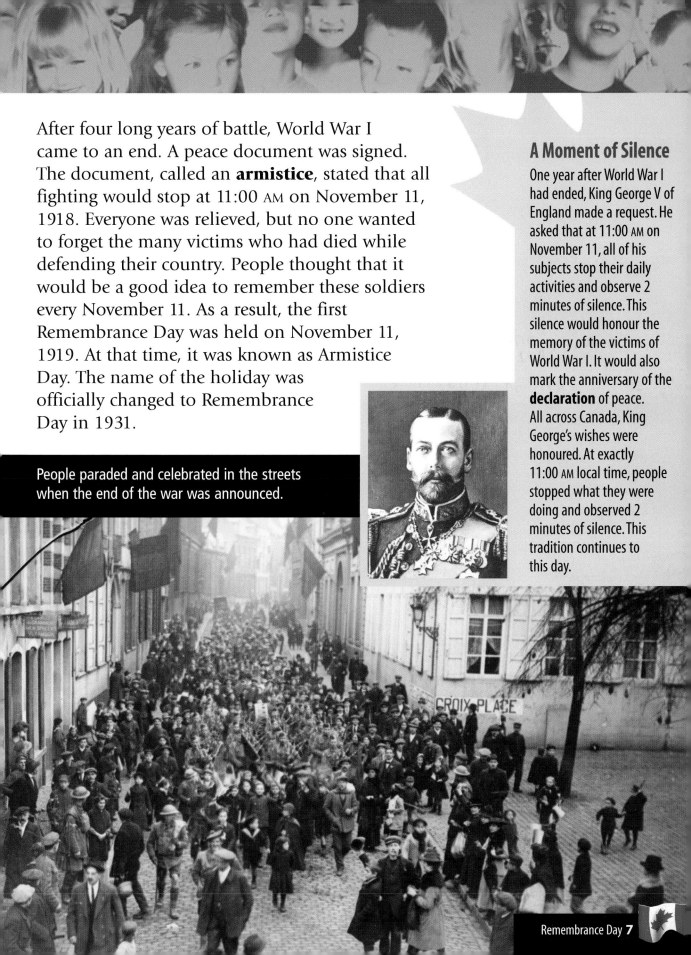

People paraded and celebrated in the streets when the end of the war was announced.

A Moment of Silence

One year after World War I had ended, King George V of England made a request. He asked that at 11:00 AM on November 11, all of his subjects stop their daily activities and observe 2 minutes of silence. This silence would honour the memory of the victims of World War I. It would also mark the anniversary of the **declaration** of peace. All across Canada, King George's wishes were honoured. At exactly 11:00 AM local time, people stopped what they were doing and observed 2 minutes of silence. This tradition continues to this day.

Times to Remember

People began to wear poppies.

Since 1919, Canada has honoured its war victims and veterans by holding special Remembrance Day ceremonies. In the 1920s and 1930s, veterans of World War I marched in parades. Canadians attended services that paid tribute to those who served in the war. Many people also began to wear poppies as a sign of remembrance. During World War I, poppies grew in the fields of France and Belgium. Many soldiers lost their lives on these fields. By wearing handmade poppies, Canadians were reminded of the many soldiers who were killed and buried in these fields.

Calgary was just one of the many Canadian cities that held veterans' parades in the years following the war.

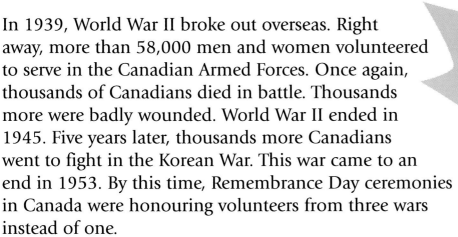

In 1939, World War II broke out overseas. Right away, more than 58,000 men and women volunteered to serve in the Canadian Armed Forces. Once again, thousands of Canadians died in battle. Thousands more were badly wounded. World War II ended in 1945. Five years later, thousands more Canadians went to fight in the Korean War. This war came to an end in 1953. By this time, Remembrance Day ceremonies in Canada were honouring volunteers from three wars instead of one.

From 1923 to 1931, Canadians celebrated Remembrance Day and Thanksgiving on the same day in November. This changed in 1931, when it was decided that Remembrance Day would always be on November 11, and Thanksgiving would be celebrated in October.

Twenty-six years after the end of World War I, Canadian troops found themselves amid the ruins of another French town.

Of the more than one million Canadians who served in World War II, about 45,000 lost their lives.

Remembrance Day Today

Ceremonies begin with a parade of war veterans.

Today, Canadians honour Remembrance Day in much the same way as they did in the past. On November 11, cities and towns across Canada hold special ceremonies. Many of these ceremonies take place at war memorials or **cenotaphs**. The ceremonies often begin with a parade of war veterans and members of the Canadian Armed Forces. Once the parade is over, a bugler plays the "Last Post." This song serves as a farewell to the men and women who died in military service. After the "Last Post," 2 minutes of silence are observed. The silence is followed by another military song, called the "Reveille." The "Reveille" reminds everyone that the memory of the dead lives on. Prayers and special poems are also recited at Remembrance Day ceremonies.

Young people play an important part in Remembrance Day ceremonies.

"The Last Post" and "Reveille" are thought to have their roots in seventeenth-century British military tradition.

In Canada, the week before Remembrance Day is called Veterans Week. It is a time when Canadians honour those who have served Canada in the causes of war and peace. During this week, veterans often visit schools and community centres to talk about their experiences.

Every year, the Royal Canadian Legion holds Remembrance Day poster, poetry, and essay contests for schools across the country. The goal of these contests is to help students understand the sacrifices that countless Canadians have made during times of war.

Prayers and poems help people remember the experiences of veterans and others who lived through the wars.

A Poem for the Fallen

War has inspired people to write poetry.

Throughout history, the horrors of war have inspired many people to write poetry. One of the most famous poems about war is called "In Flanders Fields." It was written by a Canadian army doctor named Colonel John McCrae. During World War I, Colonel McCrae cared for countless soldiers in France and Belgium. The number of soldiers who died in battle saddened him. Many of these soldiers were buried in Flanders, a city in northern Belgium.

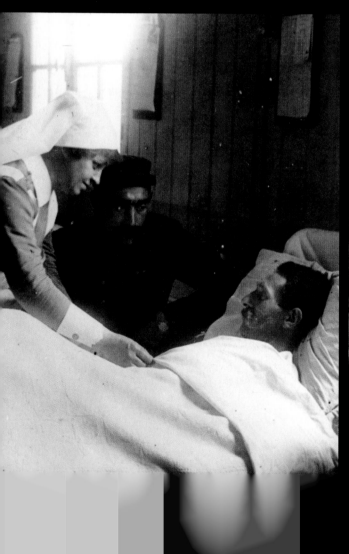

John McCrae cared for wounded soldiers on the battlefield and in hospitals like this one.

John McCrae himself was a victim of the war. He became ill and died in 1918, at a hospital in France.

When Colonel McCrae noticed that poppies were blooming around the soldiers' graves, he was inspired to write "In Flanders Fields." The poem was first published in England in 1915. It soon became very popular. People believed that the poem **symbolized** the sacrifices of those who fought in World War I. Today, "In Flanders Fields" is recited at Remembrance Day ceremonies across Canada.

People who wish to pay tribute to Colonel John McCrae can visit his childhood home in Guelph, Ontario. McCrae House is now a museum devoted to Colonel McCrae's life and work.

In Flanders Fields

In Flanders fields the poppies blow
Between the crosses, row on row,
That mark our place; and in the sky
The larks, still bravely singing, fly
Scarce heard amid the guns below.

We are the Dead. Short days ago
We lived, felt dawn, saw sunset glow,
Loved, and were loved, and now we lie
In Flanders fields.

Take up your quarrel with the foe:
To you from falling hands we throw
The torch; be yours to hold it high.
If ye break faith with us who die
We shall not sleep, though poppies grow
In Flanders fields.

Symbols of Remembrance

Symbols honour Canada's wartime dead.

Special symbols of remembrance can be found in most parts of Canada. These symbols are meant to honour the country's wartime dead. They also help to remind Canadians of the great sacrifices that many people made for their country's freedom.

The Books of Remembrance

The names of Canadians who fought and died in wartime are recorded in six special books called the Books of Remembrance. These books are on display in the Memorial Chamber of the Parliament buildings in Ottawa. Every day at 11:00 AM, a page of each book is turned. Over the course of one year, all the names in the books have been on public display. The Books of Remembrance remind us of the courage of each Canadian who fought for peace and freedom.

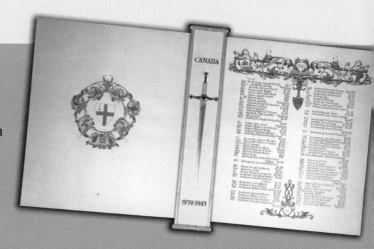

The Poppy

The red poppy is perhaps the best-known symbol of remembrance. It was chosen because of the numerous poppies that grow on the graves of fallen soldiers in Flanders. In the weeks leading up to Remembrance Day, thousands of Canadians wear a poppy on their coats or hats. The poppies are worn to honour those who died at war. In Canada, the tradition of wearing a poppy began in 1921. That year, Canada adopted the poppy as a symbol of remembrance, and as a way to raise funds for veterans in need. Today, more than $1 million are raised every year as a result of the Royal Canadian Legion's annual Poppy Campaign.

Many Canadians have been injured so badly in war that they are no longer able to work. The money raised from poppy sales provides food, shelter, and medical services for these people.

The Tomb of the Unknown Soldier

Canada's Tomb of the Unknown Soldier sits in front of the National War Memorial in Ottawa. This tomb contains the remains of an unidentified Canadian soldier who died in World War I. The soldier represents every Canadian who has died, or may die, for their country. The tomb symbolizes Canada's commitment to peace and freedom in the past, present, and future.

War Memorials and Cenotaphs

Many Canadian cities and towns have dedicated **monuments** to those who died at war. These monuments are called war memorials or cenotaphs. They are symbols of the losses suffered by Canadian communities. One of Canada's best-known memorials is the National War Memorial, which sits on Parliament Hill in Ottawa. This beautiful monument shows uniformed figures passing through an archway. The figures represent the thousands of Canadians who volunteered to fight. On Remembrance Day, thousands of people gather at the National War Memorial, and other memorials, to pay tribute to those Canadians who fought for their country.

Remembering Those Who Fought

Canadians of various cultures lost their lives in battle.

Men and women from various cultural groups served Canada in the wars of the twentieth century. Many of these Canadians lost their lives in battle. Today, Canada's ethnic groups honour their wartime dead with memorials and Remembrance Day ceremonies. On several Native **reserves** across Canada, monuments have been raised in memory of Native soldiers who died fighting for their country. Every year on November 11, residents of these reservations gather around the memorials and hold special ceremonies.

It is estimated that 12,000 Native people fought for Canada in the World Wars and in Korea.

Native-Canadian women were among those who fought for Canada.

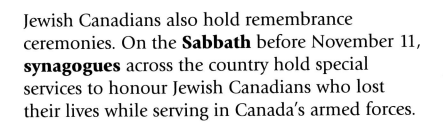

Jewish Canadians also hold remembrance ceremonies. On the **Sabbath** before November 11, **synagogues** across the country hold special services to honour Jewish Canadians who lost their lives while serving in Canada's armed forces.

Remembering Overseas

Canadians who lost their lives in wartime are honoured in countries besides Canada. All over the world, there are hundreds of memorials dedicated to the courageous Canadians who fought and died for freedom. Many of these memorials can be found on wartime battlefields in Europe, Asia, and Africa. Among the most remarkable of these memorials is the Canadian National Vimy Memorial in Vimy, France. It is located on the site of the Battle of Vimy Ridge, where Canada's greatest victory during World War I took place. The memorial was built to pay tribute to the Canadians who fought. Every November 11, Remembrance Day ceremonies are held at the Canadian National Vimy Memorial.

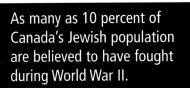

As many as 10 percent of Canada's Jewish population are believed to have fought during World War II.

Canadians Remember

P eople all across Canada observe Remembrance Day with special ceremonies. Following are just a few of the ceremonies held.

Vancouver's largest Remembrance Day ceremony takes place at Victory Square. At this ceremony, prayers and poems of remembrance are recited, and a youth choir performs wartime songs. The ceremony also features a twenty-one-gun salute. Once the service is over, war veterans and members of the Canadian Armed Forces march in a parade.

In Red Deer, Alberta, the main Remembrance Day ceremony is held at the Red Deer Arena. The event begins with a parade of veterans and members of the Canadian Armed Forces. Once the parade is over, a religious service is held.

In Saskatoon, thousands of people gather at SaskPlace for Remembrance Day. The ceremony at SaskPlace is among the largest Remembrance Day ceremonies in Canada.

Red Deer

Saskatoon

Vancouver

Canada's national Remembrance Day ceremony takes place in Ottawa, the nation's capital. Every year, more than 10,000 people gather at the National War Memorial to take part in the ceremony. Among the Canadians in attendance are the governor general and the prime minister. They deliver speeches and place wreaths of poppies in front of the memorial. The parade also features war veterans and present-day members of Canada's Armed Forces. At one point in the ceremony, fighter planes fly overhead to salute those who have died while serving in a war.

In Montréal, people gather at the city's cenotaph in Dorchester Square to take part in Remembrance Day ceremonies. Others gather at Notre-Dame-des-Neiges Cemetery to pay their respects to soldiers who are buried there.

In Sydney, Nova Scotia, surviving members of the Cape Breton Highlanders gather at a stone monument on King's Road. The monument honours the 201 members of the Highlanders who died in World War II. People at the small ceremony lay wreaths on the ground in front of the monument, and observe a moment of silence.

Sydney

Montréal

Ottawa

Remembrance Day Crafts

Remembrance day is a time to honour Canada's war veterans. These crafts can be made as a tribute to these brave men and women.

Poppy Wreath

Materials needed:
- 1 piece of cardboard
- Red construction paper
- Green marker
- Scissors
- Glue

Instructions:
1. Cut the cardboard into a circular shape. Then cut out the middle so that it resembles a wreath.
2. Take the red construction paper and cut out enough poppy shapes to cover the cardboard wreath. Colour the centre of each poppy with the green marker. (If you have cloth poppies, you can use them for this part instead.)
3. Glue the poppies onto the wreath.
4. Hang the wreath on your bedroom door or somewhere in your home. On Remembrance Day, lay the wreath at the base of a local war memorial as a symbol of your appreciation.

Thank You Card

Materials needed:
- Construction paper
- Markers or pencil crayons

Instructions:

1. Fold a piece of construction paper in half to make a card.
2. On the front of the card, draw a picture that shows your feelings about Remembrance Day.
3. On the inside of the card, write a thank you message or a poem about war and peace.
4. Send the card to your local branch of the Royal Canadian Legion.

A Remembrance Day Quiz

1 Which Canadian city is home to the Tomb of the Unknown Soldier?
a. Toronto
b. Montréal
c. Ottawa
d. Halifax

2 At what time on Remembrance Day do Canadians keep a moment of silence?
a. 10:00 AM
b. 11:00 AM
c. 12:00 AM
d. 1:00 PM

3 On which instrument is the "Last Post" usually played?

a. guitar
b. tuba
c. violin
d. bugle

5 **True or False?** Remembrance Day once had a different name.

4 **True or False?** In Canada, Remembrance Day and Thanksgiving were once celebrated on the same day.

6 **True or False?** Colonel John McCrae wrote "In Flanders Fields" during World War II.

Answers 1. c 2. b 3. d 4. True 5. True
6. False He wrote the poem during World War I.

Words to Know

armistice: an agreement to stop fighting

cenotaphs: monuments that honour victims of war

commemorate: to honour the memory of something

declaration: an announcement

monuments: buildings, statues, or other objects made to honour a person or event

peacekeeping: preserving peace between hostile nations

reserves: areas of land set aside for Canada's Native Peoples

Sabbath: a day of rest and religious observance

sacrificed: to have given up something important for the sake of something else

symbolized: something represented

synagogues: Jewish places of worship

veterans: people who have served in a war

Index